night Night
Bible Stories

PRESENTED TO

_____

BY

_____

ON THIS DATE

_____

Jesus used stories to tell all these things
to the people. He always used stories to teach people.

MATTHEW 13:34 ICB

Night Night
Bible Stories

30 STORIES FOR BEDTIME

AMY PARKER

illustrated by
VIRGINIA ALLYN

Tommy NELSON

An Imprint of Thomas Nelson
thomasnelson.com

Published in Nashville, Tennessee, by Tommy Nelson. Tommy Nelson is an imprint of Thomas Nelson. Thomas Nelson is a registered trademark of HarperCollins Christian Publishing, Inc.

Illustrated by Virginia Allyn

Tommy Nelson titles may be purchased in bulk for educational, business, fund-raising, or sales promotional use. For information, please e-mail SpecialMarkets@ ThomasNelson.com.

Scripture quotations are taken from the International Children's Bible®. Copyright © 1986, 1988, 1999 by Thomas Nelson. Used by permission. All rights reserved.

Library of Congress Cataloging-in-Publication Data is on file.

ISBN 978-1-4002-0891-3

Printed in China

19 20 21 22 23   LEO   10 9 8 7 6 5 4 3 2 1

Mfr: LEO / Heshan, China / March 2019 / PO #9522150

ALL NEW MATERIAL / Filling: POLYURETHANE FOAM / REG. NO. PA-14954 (CA), MA-3031 (CN) / MADE IN CHINA / TSSA Reg. No. 12T-1592308

To Betty and Louis, my mom and dad, who introduced
me to these stories and, in spite of everything,
gave me the rich soil in which they could grow.

And to all of the moms and dads out there—aunts,
uncles, grandparents—training up your children
in the way they should go (Proverbs 22:6),
what you are doing matters more than you know.

Contents

NEW TESTAMENT STORIES

A Letter to Parents

Dear sweet reader,

For more than a decade, parents (and grandparents and aunts and uncles and teachers and leaders) have been trusting these little Night Night books to send their little ones off to sleep with a peaceful smile. What better way to celebrate that than with a big ol' collection of Night Night Bible Stories?

In the stories that follow, you'll find your favorites, the ones that speak timeless messages of faith and love to the hearts of your little ones. Throughout, as with all of the Night Night books, you'll find the same soft tone, the same sweet illustrations, and a trusted message that helps your little ones feel safe and loved. And as always, we'll end each of these stories with a rhyme and a prayer.

We are so thankful that you've trusted us to be a part of your night night routine. And we hope this collection creates an infinitely more important trust: a trust between your little ones and the One who created them all. There is nothing sweeter or more sacred than that.

With prayers for peaceful sleep . . .

Night night,

Amy
♡

Old Testament Stories

When the World Was Made

Genesis 1-2

Way, way back, in the very beginning, everything was dark and empty. That's when the Spirit of God began to move and speak over the earth.

"Let there be light!" He said.

And just like that, the light separated from the darkness. Light was called "day." Darkness was called "night."

That was the very first day,
when the world was made.

Then God looked at the earth and saw water everywhere. So He pulled up some of the water to make the clouds in the sky. And He left some of the water down on the earth.

And that was the second day,
when the world was made.

God looked out at all of the water on the earth. It was covering everything! So He gathered the water together, and He called it "seas." When He did, there was dry land left on the rest of the earth. And God saw that this was good.

Then God said, "Grow, plants, grow! Make wheat and oats, veggies and fruit!" He even put seeds inside so the plants could keep making more plants. The dry land grew green with life, and God saw that this was very good.

And that was third day,
when the world was made.

The next day, God tossed the sun into space. He flung the moon and the stars high in the sky. "This big light, the sun, will rule the day. And the little lights, the moon and the stars, will shine at night. They will make signs and seasons, days and years." Then God saw that all of this was so, so good.

And that was the fourth day,
when the world was made.

Then God said, "Fishes, splash! Birds, fly!" And the waters burst to life with splishing and splashing. The skies began to tweet and sing. Crabs and clownfish, seahorses and sea turtles, otters and octopuses swam across seas and lakes, oceans and rivers. Cuckoos and cranes, owls and osprey spread their feathered wings and flew out over the brand-new world. God saw that this was all very good.

And that was the fifth day,
when the world was made.

On the sixth day, God said, "Animals, fill the earth!" And just like that, ants and antelopes took their first steps. Zebras strutted their stripes. Giraffes lifted their long, long necks, while monkeys stretched their arms to swing through the trees. Puppies barked, kittens purred, and the worm wriggled his way through the dirt.

It was all beautiful. It was all wonderful. What more was there to create? Oh, right—me and you!

Then God said, "Now, let's make people to be like Us. They will take care of the fish in the sea and the birds in the sky and every living thing on the earth."

And God created people in His own image. Then He blessed them, saying, "Have children so you will fill the earth and take care of it. I've given you plants and fruits to feed you and to feed the animals too."

Then God looked out at all of the beauty that He had created, and He saw that it was oh so good.

And that was the sixth day,
when the world was made.

God had made the light and the darkness,
the sky and the seas,
the sun, moon, and stars,
the plants and the trees,
fish, birds, and animals,
and you and me.

11

Sooo . . . what do you think He did next?
That's right! He *rested*.
After God had created the whole wide world, He rested.
And He blessed that day, making it a holy day.

And that was the seventh day,
when the world was made.

Dear God, thank You
for the wonderful world
You have made. And thank
You for giving us rest.
Amen.

Night night, birds, and night night, trees,
Night night, God, who made you and me.

The Big No-No

Genesis 2-3

To create the first man, God started with nothing but dust. From that dust, He formed the shape of a man. And into that shape, God breathed His very own breath. By only adding a bit of Himself to dust, God created a living, breathing man.

Yes, yes, God, make us just like You.
Yes, yes, God, make us all brand-new.

God took this man, Adam, and placed him in the beautiful garden of Eden. It was filled with plants and trees. And from those trees grew every kind of fruit and nut that God had imagined. A river ran through the middle to water the garden.

God told Adam to care for the garden and to name all of the animals. And He told Adam, "You can eat anything you want, from any tree you want. But don't eat the fruit from the Tree of the Knowledge of Good and Evil. If you do, you will die."

Well, that seemed easy enough. Adam had everything he needed right there in the garden—except one thing. God knew it wasn't good for Adam to be by himself. "I'll make someone for him," God said. And He used Adam's very own rib to create a woman, Eve.

Yes, yes, God, You give us what we need,
Yes, yes, God, just like Adam and Eve.

But one day a sneaky, slithery snake spoke to Eve. "Excusssssse me," he whispered in her ear. "God didn't really tell you that you couldn't eat the fruit from the garden . . . did He?"

"Oh, yes, we can eat the fruit," Eve said. "God told us not to eat from only *one* tree."

The snake snickered.

"If you do eat it, you will know good and evil." The snake tilted his head. "Exactly like God."

Eve looked at the tree again. It was suddenly so much more beautiful. And its fruit now looked so juicy, so sweet. And it could make her so smart.

She pulled the fruit from the tree.

No, no, Eve! Don't you take a bite!
No, no, Eve! You know what is right!

But Eve *did* take a bite. And Adam did too.

Later, in the cool of the day, God called to Adam.

"Adam, did you eat fruit from the tree I told you not to eat from?" God asked.

"Well, Eve gave me the fruit. So, yes, I did. I ate it."

Then God turned to Eve.

"The snake tricked me! He told me to!" she said.

But no matter how Adam and Eve tried to pass the blame, the truth was, they had disobeyed the one thing God had told them not to do. Adam and Eve had to leave the beautiful garden.

Before they left, God Himself made Adam and Eve clothes for the journey. And He would always be right there with them, loving them, wherever they went.

Yes, yes, God, He loves me and you,
Yes, yes, God, no matter what we do.

Thank You, God,
for loving us, even
when we disobey.
And thank You
for giving us just what
we need. Amen.

Night night, Adam, and night night, Eve,
Night night, God, who gives us what we need.

Noah Obeys (no Matter What)

Genesis 6-9

Years and years after Adam and Eve left the garden, God looked out on the earth and was very sad. Everywhere He looked, people were doing bad things.

Everyone, that is, except for Noah. Noah was a good man. No matter what, Noah obeyed God and did what was right.

"Build a boat," God told Noah. "Build it big and long and wide enough to hold you and your family and all the animals. Then I'm going to bring a flood on the earth to wash away all the bad. But your big boat will keep all of you safe."

"Okay, Lord, whatever You say.
Okay, Lord, I will obey."

So Noah went straight to work.
He built the boat just as God told him to. He put a door in

the side. He built three levels. He gathered every kind of food on the boat.

God spoke to Noah again. "Noah, it's time. Take your family and pairs of every kind of animal, and get on the boat. It's going to rain for forty days and forty nights. Everything left on earth will be washed away."

"Okay, Lord, whatever You say.
Okay, Lord, I will obey."

Suddenly animals of all kinds, from all over the place, lined up to get on the boat.

"*Rooooaaar,*" said the lions.

"*Oink, oink,*" said the pigs.

"*Chirp, chirp,*" said the crickets.

"*Tweet, tweet,*" said the birds.

Two by two, the animals boarded the big boat. Then Noah and his family got on the boat too.

It rained for forty days, and the water rose, carrying the big boat far away. After the rains stopped, the water stayed high, and Noah, his family, and the animals, rocked over the rolling waves.

Through it all, God kept Noah's family safe on the big boat. After a while, God blew a roaring wind across the water. The water went down, down, down.

Noah sent out a dove to see if there was dry land. But the dove flew around and around and finally came back to the boat. Seven days later Noah sent the dove out again. When the dove came back, it was carrying a leaf from an olive tree!

"You can come out now, Noah," God called. "Bring your wife! Bring your sons and their wives! And bring all the animals too!"

"*Rooooaaar*," said the lions.

"*Oink, oink*," said the pigs.

"*Chirp, chirp*," said the crickets.

"*Tweet, tweet*," said the birds.

As Noah and his family stood and looked at the world around them, the sky filled with a colorful rainbow.

"That rainbow is My promise," God said. "I will never again flood the earth. So go now, Noah," God told him. "Go with your family, and fill the earth again."

"Okay, Lord, whatever You say;
Okay, Lord, we will obey."

Thank You, God,
for all the animals.
And thank You for
keeping us safe in
a sometimes scary
world. Amen.

Night night, Noah, and the animals too.
Night night, God, making all things new.

Abraham's Promise

Genesis 12; 15; 17

Abraham was a faithful man. Whatever God said, Abraham believed. Whatever God asked, Abraham did. Abraham knew that God would always be true to His promises.

God's promises are always true—
For Abraham, for me and you.

But one starry night God made a promise that even Abraham found hard to believe.

"I'm going to give you a great reward," God told him.

"How can that be, God?" Abraham asked. "Even if You did give me a reward, I have no children. Who would I leave it to?"

"Abraham," God said, "look up."

Abraham lifted his eyes to the sky. A million, zillion little stars twinkled like diamonds. The wonder of God's glory was on full display.

"See those stars? You can't even count them, can you?" Abraham shook his head in awe.

"That's how many people will be in your family—too many to count," God told him. "As many as the stars in the sky."

And Abraham believed Him. Even though he was an old man, even though he had no children with his wife, even though it seemed impossible, Abraham trusted God.

God's promises are always true—
For Abraham, for me and you.

Then when Abraham was *ninety-nine* years old, God spoke to him again.

"Abraham, I'm going to give your wife a son," He began. "She will be the mother of many kings and many nations."

"But how, God?" Abraham asked Him. "Can I really have a son when I'm a hundred years old? Can Sarah really have a child when she's ninety?"

"This time next year, Sarah will have a son," God told him. "And you will name him Isaac."

Sarah laughed when she heard the news. *We're too old to have a baby*, she thought.

"Is *anything* too hard for Me to do?" God asked.

Sure enough, about a year later, Abraham and Sarah had a little baby boy. And just as God had said, they named him Isaac, which means "he laughs."

That little baby Isaac grew up to have two sons, Jacob and Esau. And Jacob grew up to have twelve sons. Those twelve sons grew into the twelve tribes of Israel. And those twelve tribes of Israel grew and grew and grew—into kings and nations, with as many people as the stars in the sky.

God's promises are always true—
For Abraham, for me and you.

Dear heavenly Father, thank
You for making the sun and
the moon and the beautiful
stars. And thank You for
always being true to Your
promises. Amen.

Night Night, Abraham and twinkling stars.
Night night, God, whose promises are ours.

Joseph the Dreamer

Genesis 37–45

Joseph was one of twelve brothers. Their mother had died when Joseph was very young, so Joseph was really close to his father. He would help his dad by telling him when his older brothers were doing something wrong. But the older brothers didn't like that very much.

As a special gift for Joseph, his dad made him a colorful coat to wear. Joseph was so proud of it. But his older brothers were jealous.

Joseph sometimes told his brothers about his dreams. "Last night I dreamed that we were all out gathering wheat and tying it together in bundles," Joseph told them. "Then my bundle stood up tall. And your bundles bowed down to mine."

"What!" the brothers cried. "Do you think we're going to bow down to you?"

Joseph's dreams made the brothers even angrier. And they came up with a plan to get rid of Joseph.

One day when they were out in the fields, some traders came by. The older brothers trapped Joseph, then sent him off to Egypt with the traders.

Don't worry, Joseph! Didn't you know?
God is with you wherever you go!

Yet while Joseph was in Egypt, God watched over him. Joseph worked for an officer of the king of Egypt. That officer trusted Joseph so much that he put him in charge of all of his household. But one day the officer's wife got mad at Joseph, and he was sent to jail.

Don't worry, Joseph! Didn't you know?
God is with you wherever you go!

Even in jail, Joseph had success. He was put in charge of all the other prisoners. One day Joseph noticed that two of the prisoners seemed sad. When he asked what was wrong, they both said that they had dreams they couldn't explain.

"Tell me your dreams," Joseph answered, "and maybe God will help me explain the dreams for you."

With God's help, Joseph was able to tell the men exactly what their dreams meant. And in just a few days, those dreams came true!

Then one day the king called for Joseph.

"I've had a dream that I don't understand," the king said. "I've been told that you can explain it to me."

"I can't explain it," Joseph said, "but God can." Joseph listened and then explained the dream to the king. "There's going to be a shortage of food, and we need to be prepared."

The king was so happy. He put Joseph in charge of storing all the food for Egypt.

After the shortage started, Joseph's brothers came looking for food. They bowed down to Joseph but didn't recognize him.

When the brothers realized that the Egyptian leader was really Joseph, they were scared. They had been so mean to their little brother. Surely Joseph would punish them!

"Don't be afraid," Joseph said to them. "What you meant to hurt me, God has used for good."

Joseph hugged his brothers and spent time with them. Then Joseph invited them and their father there to live in Egypt, where they would have everything they needed.

Don't worry, Joseph! Didn't you know?
God is with you wherever you go!

Dear God, thank You for families and forgiveness. Thank You for being with us wherever we go. Amen.

Night night, Joseph, who dreamed so big,
Who chose to trust, who chose to forgive.

Splitting the Sea

Exodus 2–15

At the time when Moses was born, Hebrews were treated very badly by the king of Egypt, called the pharaoh. To protect Moses, his Hebrew mother placed him in a basket and hid him at the edge of the water. Pharaoh's daughter found Moses and took him home to be raised in the palace.

Later, when Moses was a young man, he got into some trouble. He ran far away from Egypt, planning never to return. But soon God called to him from a burning bush.

"Moses!"

"Yes?" Moses said to the bush.

"My people, the Hebrews, are being treated badly," God said from the flames. "I want you to go to Egypt to save them from the pharaoh."

"Me?" Moses asked. "God, I'm nobody. How can I save Your people?"

"Because I will help you," God answered.

Go, go, Moses, you know what you should do.
Go, go, Moses—God will be with you!

With that, Moses and his brother, Aaron, made the journey back to Egypt. They went to the pharaoh and told him, "God said, 'Let My people go!'"

"No way!" Pharaoh answered. "I'm not letting all these people go!"

So God sent all kinds of bad things to convince Pharaoh to let the Hebrews go. First, God made all the water turn yucky. Then He sent herds and herds of hopping frogs. He sent storms and sickness.

Finally, Pharaoh begged Moses, "Please, all of you Hebrews, get out of here! I will let you go. Just leave us alone!"

Then all God's people packed up and left Egypt. As they walked, God led the way, using a big cloud during the day and a tall pillar of fire at night.

But Pharaoh changed his mind. He had made the Hebrews do all the hard work in Egypt. Who would do the work after they were gone? So he sent his soldiers to chase after the Hebrews.

Moses and the Hebrews reached the edge of the Red Sea. People were yelling. Children were crying. Sheep were *baa*-ing. In front of Moses was nothing but water. Behind him was the thundering of Pharaoh's horses and chariots. Had God brought him this far only to leave him now?

Go, go, Moses, you know what you should do.
Go, go, Moses—God will be with you!

"Don't be scared!" Moses yelled over the noise. "God is fighting for us. Just watch and see!"

Then Moses closed his eyes and
stretched out his hand over the water.
When he did, a great wind blew
over the water. The waves rippled,
and the water began to split in
two. The people watched, amazed.
Right down the center of the
Red Sea, a dry path formed. And
with walls of water standing on

each side of them, the Hebrews, God's people, walked on dry land to the other side. Then the path closed up, keeping the soldiers from following them.

Moses found himself at the edge of the water again. People were singing. Children were cheering. Sheep were *baa*-ing. Behind him was nothing but water.

And in front of him was freedom and the great land God had promised to His people.

Go, go, Moses, you know what you should do.
Go, go, Moses—God will be with you!

Thank You, God, for taking care of Your people. And thank You for making a way when it seems there is nowhere to go. Amen.

Night night, Moses, and God's people too.
May God be with you, whatever you do.

A Donkey Talks

Numbers 22–24

King Balak looked out over the plains, terrified. The Hebrews who had left Egypt were traveling through his country of Moab. There were thousands and thousands of them camping there.

"They're going to eat everything we have!" the king said to the elders. Then he came up with a plan. "There's a man named Balaam. Whenever he curses or blesses someone, it happens. Go to him, pay him, and ask him to come and put a curse on the Hebrews."

So the king's leaders did as he asked.

Balaam answered them, "Stay here for the night. Tomorrow I will tell you what the Lord says."

"Lead on, Lord. Show me the way.
Help me to see. Help me to obey."

In the night, God came to Balaam and said, "Do not go with these men. Do not put a curse on the Hebrews, the people of Israel. They are My blessed people."

The next morning, Balaam told the king's leaders, "Go back home. I cannot go with you."

The leaders went back and told the king what Balaam had said.

"Go back to him!" the king ordered. "Tell him we'll pay him whatever he wants. Just get him to come and put a curse on these people!"

They did as the king said. But Balaam answered, "The king could give me his entire palace and all the gold and silver in it. I still can't disobey God. But stay here for the night, and I'll see what God says."

"Lead on, Lord. Show me the way.
Help me to see. Help me to obey."

That night God told Balaam, "You can go with them. But do only as I tell you to."

So the next morning, Balaam went with the men. But as they were traveling, an angel of the Lord who was holding a sword stood in the road to stop Balaam from going any farther. Only Balaam's donkey could see the angel, and it swerved off into a field. Balaam swatted the donkey to get it back onto the path.

The angel of the Lord appeared again. This time, the angel stood on a small path between two walls. The donkey saw the angel and ran into the wall, smashing Balaam's foot. Balaam got mad and swatted the donkey again.

A little farther ahead, the angel stood in a space that was too narrow for them to go around. So this time, the donkey just lay down in the middle of the road with Balaam sitting on top. This made Balaam so angry that he swatted the donkey with a stick.

That's when God gave Balaam's donkey a voice. "Why do you keep hitting me?" the donkey asked Balaam. "What have I done?"

Balaam answered the donkey. "You swerved into a field. You crushed my foot. And now you're lying in the middle of the road, making me look dumb!"

The donkey answered, "Have you ever seen me act this way?"

"Hmm, no, I haven't."

And suddenly, Balaam understood. Balaam could see the angel of the Lord standing in the road with his sword drawn.

The angel said, "Three times, I stood here to stop you. Three times, your donkey saw me, but you did not. And three times, your donkey turned away from me and saved your life."

"I'm so sorry!" Balaam cried. "Tell me what I should do."

And with God's direction, Balaam kept gong with the men that day. But he did not curse the people of Israel, God's people, as King Balak wanted him to do. Balaam *blessed* them. Even though it made the king very angry, Balaam stood on a mountain overlooking the Israelites, and he blessed them *three* times—just as God had told him to do.

"Lead on, Lord. Show me the way.
Help me to see. Help me to obey."

Thank You, God,
for caring enough
about us to show us
the right way
to go. Help me always
look for You to lead
the way. Amen.

Night night, Balaam, and his donkey too,
Who saw God's way and followed Him through.

Joshua and the Big Wall

Joshua 6

God's people had spent a long time walking. Now they were finally ready to enter the promised land. It was a land with plenty of food, filled with grapes so big and juicy that they could almost taste them. There was just one problem: a humongous stone wall separated the people from the city.

Joshua wasn't sure what to do. Moses had just passed away, and now Joshua was the leader of the Israelites, God's people. But if Joshua knew anything at all, he knew that God would take care of them.

"I have given you this city," God reminded Joshua. Then He told Joshua exactly what to do. "Take your army and the priests, and march around the city. March around it once a day, every day, for six days. Then on the seventh day, march around the city seven times. When the priests give a long blast on their trumpets, tell everyone to give a loud shout.
Then the walls will fall."

Hmm, how exactly would that work? Marching and shouting to knock down a big ol' wall? The plan may have sounded silly, but Joshua prepared the people to do exactly as God had said.

"March, march! March, march! That is what we'll do! March, march! March, march! 'Cause He told us to!"

Joshua gathered the army and told them to collect their weapons. He called the priests and asked them to bring their trumpets. Then Joshua carefully explained the plan just how God had explained it to him. And with that, the people were ready.

On the first day, Joshua, the army, and the priests marched around the wall. After one march around the city, they went back to their camp for the night. On the second day, they marched again, and then the third, and the fourth, and every day for six days in a row.

That big ol' wall didn't budge. But still . . .

"March, march! March, march! That is what we'll do!
March, march! March, march! 'Cause He told us to!"

On the seventh day, as soon as the sun peeked over the
mountains, the Israelites were ready. Seven times, they marched
around that city. On the seventh round, seven priests blew seven
trumpets. Then all of God's people gave a faithful shout.

First there was a rumble . . . and then a tumble . . . and then
a great big *CRAAASH!*

As silly as the plan may have seemed, the marching,
the trumpet-blowing, and the shouting of God's
faithful people brought that big wall down
to the ground. And just beyond the pile
of rubble was the promised land,
the land with plenty of food,
filled with grapes so
big and juicy that
they could almost
taste them. It was
right there, waiting
for them, just as
God had
promised.

"March, march! March, march! That is what we'll do!
March, march! March, march! 'Cause He told us to!"

Dear God, thank You for having a plan for Your people. Help me always follow Your ways, no matter how different they may seem. Amen.

Night night, Joshua, such a faithful man,
Leading God's people, following God's plan.

The Wimpy Warrior

Judges 6-7

Gideon was just a little guy. But he did what he could to help his family.

One day he was in a small room taking the grains off the long stalks of wheat so his family could eat it. He had to hide from the Midianites while he did this, or else they would come and take his family's food.

While Gideon was hiding and harvesting, an angel from God appeared, saying, "God is with you, mighty warrior!"

Gideon looked around. *Mighty warrior?*

"Sir, if God is with us," Gideon began, "then why is everyone trying to take everything we have? God has always been there to save His people. But not anymore."

That's when God spoke to Gideon. "I'm sending *you* to save your people from the Midianites."

"Me, Lord?" Gideon asked. "My family is the weakest in the whole country. And *I* am the weakest in my whole family!"

"Trust Me, Gideon—together, we are strong.
Trust Me, Gideon—I've been here all along."

So Gideon began gathering men, trying to make an army big enough to fight the Midianites. He gathered and gathered until he had more than thirty thousand men!

"Wait, Gideon," God said to him. "You have too many men."

Gideon was confused. If he was going to fight the Midianites, he was going to need every single one of those men.

"I want My people to know without a doubt that I saved them," God answered. "If any of the men are afraid, tell them that they can go home."

So Gideon did. And twenty-two thousand men went home.

But God said, "Gideon, there are still too many men. Take them to the stream to drink. If they get down on their knees to drink, send them home. If they cup the water in their hands and lap it up like dogs, they can stay."

Thousands of men got on their knees to drink from the stream. And Gideon sent them home.

That night, Gideon stood on the hill with only three hundred men, looking down at the valley where the Midianites camped. There were so many of them! How could Gideon defeat them with only three hundred men?

"Trust Me, Gideon—together, we are strong.
Trust Me, Gideon—I've been here all along."

God gave Gideon a plan. Gideon rounded up all the clay
jars and trumpets that his
army had. Then he dropped
burning torches inside
the jars.

62

"Okay, men! Grab a jar. Grab a trumpet. And do what I do!"
The men followed Gideon, tiptoeing above the quiet
Midianite camp.

When everyone was in place, Gideon held his torch high,
smashed a jar to the ground, and blew into that trumpet with a
mighty blast. Then Gideon's three hundred men did the same.

All that smashing and blasting woke the Midianites from
their sleep. They came scurrying out of their tents like
mice, shouting and screaming. When they ran
into one another, they thought they were
being attacked. So they began fighting!
Gideon and his three hundred men
simply stood on the hill and watched.
They didn't have to do anything to defeat
the Midianites. The Midianites defeated
themselves.

"Trust Me, Gideon—together, we are strong.
Trust Me, Gideon—I've been here all along."

Thank You, God,
for loving us and
fighting for us, even
when we are weak.
Please help me
remember that with
You, I am strong.
Amen.

Night night, Gideon, and the three hundred men
who trusted God to help His people again.

God Calls Samuel

I Samuel 1–3

For years and years Hannah and her husband were not able to have children. It made her so sad to think that she would never hold her baby in her arms or watch her little one grow.

One day she cried out to God, asking Him to please give her a child. She promised God that if He did, she would let that child serve Him forever.

"Speak, speak, Lord. I'll be here when You call.
Speak, speak, Lord. I'll give You my all."

Several months after that prayer, Hannah and her husband had a little boy named Samuel. Her prayers had been answered!

As Samuel grew, Hannah rocked him and held him close. She watched in awe as his five tiny fingers wrapped around hers. She treasured every giggle, every coo. She took pride in each tiny footstep.

But soon it was time. Hannah packed a bag for Samuel, and they traveled back to the place where she had first prayed for this child. She explained to Eli, the priest, that her son belonged to God. And Eli welcomed Samuel into his new home in God's holy tent.

As Hannah left, she began to sing thanks to God for the joy He had given her. And she returned to visit Samuel regularly, making new clothes for him as he grew.

After some time, Samuel felt right at home there in the holy tent with Eli the priest. And one night as Samuel was lying in bed, he heard a voice calling him.

"Samuel . . ."

Samuel ran to Eli. "Yes, Eli? You called me."

"I didn't call you, son," Eli answered. "Go back to bed."

"Samuel . . . Samuel!"

The voice was loud and clear. Samuel ran to Eli again. "Eli, you called me."

"No, I didn't," Eli answered, confused. "Go back to bed."

Samuel had barely gotten back into bed when heard the voice a third time. He ran back to Eli. "Sir, I am here. You called me."

"Ah yes, Samuel. Someone *is* calling you." Eli smiled. "But it's not me. The next time you hear the voice, say, 'Speak, Lord. I'm listening.'"

Samuel slowly walked back to bed. Now he was the one confused. He lay there, barely blinking, listening to the quiet.

"Speak, speak, Lord. I'll be here when You call. Speak, speak, Lord. I'll give You my all."

"Samuel . . . Samuel!"

Samuel sat straight up in bed. "Speak, Lord. I'm listening."

And right then, right there, young Samuel talked with God Himself. God told Samuel about His plans for the future, about His plans for His people. And Samuel listened.

After that, God continued to speak to Samuel throughout his entire life. And Samuel became known throughout Israel as a great prophet of the Lord. Sometimes God spoke to Samuel out loud, and sometimes He spoke to Samuel through His written Word. But no matter how God spoke, no matter when He called, Samuel listened.

"Speak, speak, Lord. I'll be here when You call.
Speak, speak, Lord. I'll give You my all."

Dear heavenly
Father, thank You
for always listening
to us when we call
on You. Please help
us always listen
when You call us too.
Amen.

Night night, Samuel, and Hannah too.
You prayed and listened when God spoke to you.

The Great Big Meanie

1 Samuel 17

In the town of Bethlehem, a man named Jesse had eight sons.

The three oldest sons were fighting in the Israelite army with King Saul. Their camp was on one hill and the Philistine army was on the other, with a valley between them. As the men readied for battle, the Philistines sent out their biggest, baddest guy: a super-warrior named Goliath.

Goliath was more than nine feet tall. He wore a bronze helmet on his head and a full coat of scaly armor on his chest. His legs were also covered with bronze, and he carried a bronze spear on his back. He looked like a giant metal dragon!

Every single day for forty days, Goliath stomped out to the middle of the valley.

Boom-clank, boom-clank, BOOM!

"Just send one guy out to fight me!" Goliath would yell at the Israelites. "If he can beat me, you win!"

But the Israelites would all run and hide. *There's no way any of us can defeat that giant!* they thought.

About this time, back at home, Jesse called for his youngest son, David, who was out watching the sheep. Jesse packed some bread, grain, and cheese. "Take this to your brothers," he told David. "Then come back and let me know if they're okay."

When David got to the valley where the armies were, he couldn't believe what he saw. There was a big ol' bully out there threatening God's army.

"Who does he think he is?" David said to the Israelite men. "And why does he think he can defeat God's people?"

"Hey, you big ol' meanie! Yes, you may be tall,
But my God is bigger—the biggest of them all!"

King Saul heard about what David had said and asked to speak to him.

"Let me at him!" David said to the king. "I will fight this Philistine."

"But you're just a boy," King Saul said.

"Maybe so," David began, "but when I was taking care of the sheep and a bear came, I would chase it away. And when a lion came, I saved the sheep from its mouth. God has protected me from lions and bears. He will protect me from this giant too."

"Go then," King Saul said, "and may God be with you."

Young David tried on King Saul's armor, but he couldn't even walk in it. So he took it off, walked over to a nearby stream, and picked up five smooth stones. He gripped his sling and walked out to meet the giant.

"What is this?" Goliath bellowed. "Are you using a stick to fight me, like I'm a dog?"

But David stood tall. "You may have a sword and a spear," he shouted at the giant, "but I come in the name of the Lord!"

Goliath took a step forward, and David ran right at him. He placed a stone in his sling and flung it directly at the giant's forehead.

Whoosh. Pow. SPLAT.

The towering warrior wobbled, then fell flat on his face. The Philistines took off running. And the Israelites went running after them.

"Hey, you big ol' meanie! Yes, you may be tall,
But my God is bigger—the biggest of them all!"

Dear God, thank You for always standing up for me. Help me stand up for You too. Amen.

Night night, David, and God's people too—
When you fight for God, God will fight for you!

The World's Wisest King

I Kings 3-4

The boy David who defeated Goliath grew up to be the king of Israel. Then King David had a son of his own and named him Solomon. When it was time for King David to pass down the job of king, David gave that job to his son Solomon.

King Solomon loved God and followed all His commands. But he knew that in order to lead God's people well, he would need help.

"Please, Lord, guide me—show me what to do.
Please, Lord, guide me—make me wise like You."

One night after King Solomon had been to worship, God spoke to him in a dream. "Solomon, you can ask Me for anything you want," God said. "I will give it to you."

"Oh, God, You were so good to my father. Now You've allowed me to take his place as king," Solomon replied. "But I'm young. I don't have his wisdom. Please, give me wisdom so I can rule Your people the way You want me to."

"Please, Lord, guide me—show me what to do. Please, Lord, guide me—make me wise like You."

"You could have asked for so many things," God said to Solomon. "But you asked for wisdom to lead My people. Because of this, I'll give you what you asked for. But I'll also give you what you didn't ask for. You will have wisdom, riches, and honor unlike anyone else to ever live."

And so it was.

Solomon was a wise and fair king. He also taught the people about trees and plants, about birds, animals, and fish. He left behind thousands of wise sayings and songs. And there were peace and great riches in his kingdom for his entire life.

Because Solomon wanted what was best for God's people, God gave him that—and so much more.

"Please, Lord, guide me—show me what to do.
Please, Lord, guide me—make me wise like You."

Thank You, God, for Your great wisdom. Please help me trust that You always know what is best. Amen.

Night night, Solomon, who wanted what was best. He asked only for wisdom and let God do the rest.

The World's Bravest Queen

The Book of Esther

A beautiful young girl named Esther lived in Persia. Because she had no parents, her cousin, Mordecai, raised her. He loved her and protected her as his own daughter until she grew to be a young woman.

King Xerxes was the king of Persia, and he was looking for a queen. He sent his servants all over the country to look for beautiful young women to be his wife. When the king's men saw Esther, they were amazed by her beauty and took her back to the palace.

Beautiful Esther, part of God's plan.
Brave, young Esther, God's helping hand.

The girls who were chosen were taken to meet the king. King Xerxes liked Esther the most. He chose her to be his queen, and she came to live in his beautiful palace.

But a mean man named Haman worked for the king. He wanted to destroy all the Jews in Persia. Haman didn't know it, but Esther, the queen, was also a Jew.

Mordecai sent Esther a message. "You have to do something to save our people!"

"But I can't!" Esther sent a message back. "No one is allowed to go see the king unless he calls them."

"Esther, you have to. It's the only way to save your people—to save yourself," Mordecai said. "Who knows? Maybe you were made queen for this very reason."

Beautiful Esther, part of God's plan.
Brave, young Esther, God's helping hand.

Esther knew that Mordecai was right. So she prayed.
Mordecai prayed. And after three days, Esther dressed up in her
royal clothes and went to see the king.

When the king saw her, he called her in. "Queen Esther,
what do you need? Whatever it is, I will give it to you."

"Please," Esther began, "will you and Haman come to a banquet with me today?"

The king agreed. Then at dinner, he said, "Okay, my queen, what do you need? What can I give you?"

"I would like . . ." Esther began, but she got nervous. "I would like for you both to come to dinner with me tomorrow night."

"Okay . . ." the king answered, "tomorrow night!"

The next night Queen Esther, the king, and Haman sat down to eat again. "Now tell me, Queen Esther," the king asked again, "what can I do for you?"

"Please," she began bravely, "please just let me and my people live."

"What do you mean?" King Xerxes asked. "Who would dare to hurt you or your people?"

Queen Esther slowly pointed at Haman. "He would."

"What! Take Haman away!" the king ordered his men.

And as for Queen Esther, Mordecai, and their people—God's people— they were saved from Haman's evil plan. They were saved . . .

all because a brave, young queen stepped up and stepped into God's purpose even when she was scared.

Beautiful Esther, part of God's plan.
Brave, young Esther, God's helping hand.

Thank You, God, for having a plan for my life. Help me be brave enough to follow it. Amen.

Night night, Esther, and Mordecai too,
Who trusted in God to see them through.

Daniel Is Safe

Daniel 6

Daniel was one of King Darius's most trusted men. Daniel also was the best worker of them all. So King Darius planned to put Daniel in charge of everyone—the entire kingdom!

But when the other men heard about King Darius's plan, they were jealous. And they came up with a plan of their own—a plan to get rid of Daniel.

"Watch him," one of the men said. "Surely we can catch him doing something wrong."

They watched and they watched. But again and again, Daniel proved to be a hard worker who could be trusted by everyone.

Finally, one of the men laughed and said, "I've got an idea . . ."

All of the men—except Daniel—went together to the king. "Oh, King Darius! You're so wonderful that we want you to make a law to honor your great wonderfulness. For the next thirty days, no one can pray to anyone—except to you, our most wonderfulest king."

"Okay," the king said.

"And if someone does," the men added, "he will be thrown into the lions' den."

And the law was made.

It wasn't long before Daniel heard about the new law. But Daniel knew that God's law was more important than the king's law.

"Laugh, laugh, rulers—I know the law you made.
Roar, roar, lions—I am not afraid."

So as always, Daniel went up to his room, got down on his knees, and prayed.

The men were watching Daniel through his window. As soon as they saw him praying, they went straight to the king.

"Oh, wonderful king," the men tattled, "didn't you make a law that said no one could pray to anyone but you?"

"Yes," the king answered.

"And doesn't that law say that anyone who disobeys will be thrown into the lions' den?"

"Yes, yes," the king answered.

"Well, Daniel is not following the law. He's still praying to his God three times a day!"

"Oh no!" The king didn't mean for the law to hurt Daniel. He tried everything he could to save Daniel from the punishment. But once the king made a law, it could not be changed. Sadly, King Darius gave the order for Daniel to be taken to the den full of lions.

"I hope that your God can save you!" the king said. Then his men threw Daniel in with the lions and put a big stone over the opening of the lions' den.

"Laugh, laugh, rulers—I know the law you made.
Roar, roar, lions—I am not afraid."

That night King Darius could not eat. He could not sleep. The next morning, as soon as the sun began to rise, the king ran back to the lions' den.

"Daniel, Daniel!" the king shouted. "Has your God saved you?"

"Yes, King Darius!" came a voice from the lions' den. "He sent an angel to keep me safe all night long!"

"Get him out of there!" the king ordered. And the king's men lifted Daniel, who did not have a single scratch, from the depths of the lions' den.

Daniel had obeyed the laws of God, even when the king's law said it was wrong. And God saved Daniel—even when the king could not.

After that, King Darius made a new law. Everyone must respect Daniel's God, the God who saved Daniel from the lions' den.

"Laugh, laugh, rulers—I know the law you made.
Roar, roar, lions—I am not afraid."

Thank You, God,
for always loving me
and protecting me.
Please help me obey
You, even when it is
scary. Amen.

Night night, Daniel, and the lions too.
When you obey God, He protects you.

Jonah Doesn't Obey (At First)

The Book of Jonah

Jonah was a prophet of God. This means God gave Jonah messages, and Jonah delivered them wherever God told him to go. But Jonah didn't always act the way a prophet should.

One time God told Jonah, "I need you to go to Nineveh. They're doing awful things. Tell them to stop."

But Jonah took off running in the other direction, far, far away from Nineveh. He found a boat that was going in the opposite direction, paid his way, and climbed on board.

Silly, silly Jonah! Don't you run away!
Silly, silly Jonah—it's better to obey!

Jonah went to take a nap. But while he slept, the winds picked up. The waves grew strong. And the boat began to rock.

"You! Hey!" one of the sailors shouted at him. "Get up and pray! Pray for your God to save us!"

Jonah blinked and looked around. Everything was spinning, tossing, and turning.

Crack! went the boards overhead.

Whoosh! went the waves outside.

"Aaaaaaagh!" went the sailors on deck.

Jonah stepped up to face the men. He knew that this was all his fault.

"Who are you?" the men asked Jonah. "Why is this happening to us?"

"I am a Hebrew," Jonah explained. "I worship the God of heaven, the God who made land and sea."

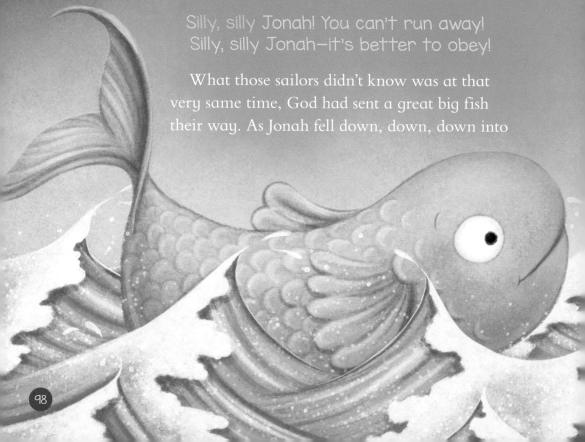

"Okay, then," the men asked, "how do we make the sea *stop?*"

Jonah looked down and mumbled, "Throw me overboard."

"What?" the men asked. "It sounded like you said to throw overboard."

"Yes." Jonah looked up at them. "Throw me into the sea."

The men looked at Jonah. Then they looked at each other. Finally, they gave in. "God, please don't punish us," they said. Then they threw Jonah over the side of the boat.

Silly, silly Jonah! You can't run away!
Silly, silly Jonah—it's better to obey!

What those sailors didn't know was at that very same time, God had sent a great big fish their way. As Jonah fell down, down, down into

the ocean, that big fish scooped him up in his mouth and swallowed him whole.

And that's where Jonah stayed—in that stinky, smelly fish's belly for three whole days and nights. This gave him plenty of time to think. And to pray. And to say, "I'm sorry."

On the third day, that big ol' fish swam up to the shore and spit Jonah out—right onto dry land.

Then God gave His instructions again. "Get up, Jonah. Go to Nineveh. Tell them what I said."

This time, Jonah obeyed. And the people of Nineveh were saved.

Silly, silly Jonah! You can't run away!
Silly, silly Jonah—it's better to obey!

Holy God, thank You
for having rules that
keep us safe. Help
me follow those
rules. Amen.

Night night, Jonah, and Nineveh too!
When you listen to God, He will save you!

New Testament Stories

An Angel Visits Mary and Joseph

Matthew 1; Luke 1

In the town of Nazareth, a girl named Mary was engaged to marry a man named Joseph.

Joseph was from the family of David. That's the same David who defeated Goliath many years earlier. And it's the same family from which Jesus, the Savior of the world, was expected to come!

Mary probably wasn't thinking about any of that, though. She was just a normal girl in a normal town, getting ready to marry a normal guy. At least, she *was*—until the angel came to her.

"Greetings!" the angel said to Mary. "God is with you!"
Mary blinked.

"Don't be scared," the angel continued. "God is happy with you! You're going to have a Son. Name Him Jesus."

"But I—I'm not even married yet," Mary finally said.

The angel smiled. "Anything is possible with God. No one thought your cousin Elizabeth would have a baby, and she's going to have a son too," the angel explained. "Besides, this baby isn't like other babies. This baby is God's own Son."

Mary, Mary,
God's favored one,
Chosen to carry
God's own Son.

Mary was still a little scared. And she was still a little confused. But she knew what she must do.

"I serve the Lord," she said to the angel. "Let this happen, just as you said it would."

Then as quickly as the angel had appeared, he was gone.

And Mary quickly left too—to visit her cousin Elizabeth.

"Elizabeth!" Mary called as she got close to her cousin's house.

Elizabeth came out, running toward her. "You are blessed, Mary! God has blessed you and the baby you're going to have!"

How could Elizabeth know? Mary had just found out herself!

"When I heard you call," Elizabeth continued, "the baby in my belly jumped with joy!"

Mary, Mary,
God's favored one,
Chosen to carry
God's own Son.

But there was one other person who needed to know: Joseph. When he found out that Mary was going to have a baby, he was sad and confused. How could he marry Mary if she was already going to have a baby?

Joseph fell asleep, worrying about these things. And that's when an angel visited him too.

"Joseph," the angel said to him, "take Mary as your wife. The baby is from the Holy Spirit. Name Him Jesus, because He will save people from their sins."

Joseph woke up, relieved. And he did just as the angel said. He married Mary.

Mary, Mary, God's favored one,
Chosen to carry God's own Son.

Heavenly Father, thank You for using people like me in Your great big plans. Help me say yes whenever You call. Amen.

Night night, Mary, and Joseph too.
You both said yes when God called you.

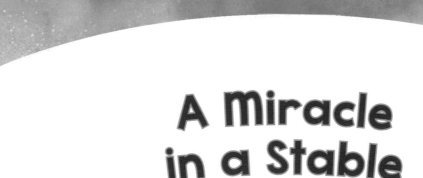

A Miracle in a Stable

Luke 2

Before Jesus was born, the emperor ordered everyone to go back to their hometowns to be counted. This meant that Mary and Joseph would have to go all the way to Bethlehem, which was Joseph's hometown.

By this time, Mary was almost ready to have baby Jesus. As the baby grew bigger and bigger in her belly, it was harder and harder for her to walk around comfortably. But walking for a whole week, all the way to Bethlehem? That would be really difficult for Mary.

But they had to go. So Joseph loaded up a donkey to carry what they would need. Then—*clip-clop, clip-clop*—they made the long trip to Bethlehem.

When they got there, it was very crowded because everyone else from Bethlehem was there to be counted too. Joseph tried to find them a nice place to stay where Mary could be comfortable and rest. But there were no rooms left anywhere. So Mary and Joseph stayed in a room where animals were kept.

Soon it was time—the time that Mary and Joseph had been waiting for ever since that angel came. Right then, right there, among the braying donkeys and *baa*-ing sheep, the Savior of the world was born. And they named Him Jesus, just as the angel had said.

> A gift of grace, this holy One,
> A gift of love, God's own Son.

Mary wrapped the tiny baby in soft cloths. She laid him in the softest bed she could find, which was an animal feeding box that was filled with hay. And together, Mary and Joseph and the animals, too, gazed in awe at the miracle that lay before them.

Jesus. Immanuel. God with us.

The ordinary had met the most extraordinary. The King of kings lay in a bed of animals' hay. And a tiny baby would soon become the Savior of the world.

Heaven had come to earth, and it would never be the same.

A gift of grace, this holy One,
A gift of love, God's own Son.

Dear heavenly Father,
thank You for the
precious gift of Your
Son, Jesus. Help me
remember always that
He is Immanuel, "God
with us." Amen.

Night night, Jesus, in a bed made of hay,
The One who would save the world someday!

Angels in the Sky

Luke 2

Just outside of Bethlehem, around the same time when Jesus was born, shepherds were out in the fields with their sheep. It was a beautiful night under the stars.

Sheep were *baa*-ing. Shepherds were snoring. Then suddenly, from out of nowhere, there came a burst of bright, white light. And in the middle of all the light, there stood what looked like a man. But it was not a man. It was . . . an angel.

The shepherds stumbled, shielded their eyes, and stared.

"It's okay. Don't be scared," the angel said. "I'm here to bring news—the best news—for everyone in the world!"

Still, the shepherds did not take their eyes off the angel.

"Today, there in Bethlehem," the angel pointed, "your Savior was born. He is the Messiah, the Christ, the Lord." The shepherds looked at each other. Could it really be true? The Messiah? The One the prophets told about? The One that their parents and grandparents had taught them about? The Promised One sent from God to save the world?

The angel smiled. "Just look for the brand-new baby wrapped in soft cloths. He'll be sleeping in the hay in the animals' feeding trough."

With that, a blinding light burst across the sky, lighting up the fields, outshining the brilliant stars. There were angels—so many angels! All together, in one beautiful, powerful voice, the angels began to praise God.

"Glory to God, peace on the earth,
This is the night of the Savior's birth!"

Soon the light faded, the voices softened, and the angels disappeared back into the heavens from which they came.

The shepherds just stood there, still staring at the sky in silence. Finally, one spoke up. "Let's go," he said trembling. "Let's go see Him!"

All at once, the shepherds scrambled toward Bethlehem to find the baby. It wasn't long until they were pointed toward a small, quiet animal stable. They tiptoed in and saw

Him, just as the angels had said. He was wrapped in cloth and lying in a bed of hay.

"Um, excuse us," one of the shepherds said to Mary and Joseph. "But you'll never believe what happened."

Mary and Joseph looked at each other and smiled.

The shepherds took turns telling Mary and Joseph all about the first angel and then the whole group of angels. They told about their beautiful voices and their brilliant light. They explained how the angel described Jesus and how they found Him.

Mary listened to every word. And she knew in her heart that this was just the beginning.

The shepherds walked out of the stable praising God and thanking Him for the glorious gift He had given them. The angels had shared a heavenly secret, giving them a personal invitation to come sit in the presence of this King of kings, this holy child.

But it wouldn't be a secret for long. . . .

"Glory to God, peace on the earth,
This is the night of the Savior's birth!"

Holy Father, thank You
for inviting us to see Your
glory for ourselves. Help
us always believe You and
go right where You lead.
Amen.

Night night, shepherds, rejoicing still,
Of how heaven came down there in the fields.

Jesus in His Father's House

Luke 2

As Jesus grew, God took care of Mary, Joseph, and their family. Just like other children His age, Jesus grew tall and strong. But He had a wisdom all His own.

Every year Jesus and His family traveled from their home in Nazareth to Jerusalem to celebrate the Passover Feast. It was a special feast remembering how God had saved His people from Egypt with Moses.

When Jesus was twelve years old, His family went to Jerusalem as they always did. They celebrated the Passover, then headed home. As usual, Mary and Joseph traveled with other families and friends from their area. And as usual, the older children walked and talked and played together as they went.

After a day of walking, Mary and Joseph realized they hadn't seen Jesus in a while. They looked all around them. They asked family and friends. But Jesus was nowhere to be found.

"Jesus, Jesus,
where could You be?
Jesus, Jesus,
stay right here with me."

That's when they realized that they hadn't seen Jesus since they were in Jerusalem! Immediately, Mary and Joseph turned around and headed back. How could this have happened? How could they have lost God's own Son?

It took Mary and Joseph a whole day to get back to
Jerusalem. Once they were in the city, they looked everywhere,
asked everyone. But Jesus was nowhere to be found.

"Jesus, Jesus,
where could You be?
Jesus, Jesus,
stay right here with me."

Then on the third day, just like that, there He was.

His mother gasped when she saw Him. His father, Joseph, watched in awe. As happy as they were to have found Him, they were just as surprised at what He was doing. At twelve years old, Jesus sat there with the teachers in the temple, looking and sounding almost like a teacher Himself.

Mary ran to Him. "Jesus!" she cried. "We've been looking for You for *three* days! *Three* days! Why would You do this to us?"

Jesus looked up at His mother and said, "But, Mom, didn't you know that I would be in My Father's house?"

Mary blinked. She looked at Joseph. He just answered with a shrug. They weren't really sure what Jesus meant by that. But they sure were happy to have Him back.

Jesus, Jesus, I know where You'll be.
Jesus, Jesus, right here with me.

Dear God, thank You for being our
Father in heaven. Help us always want
to be right where You are. Amen.

Night night, Jesus, who's never really gone,
He's both here and with His Father,
right where He belongs.

Follow, Follow Me!

Mark 1–2

When Mary's cousin Elizabeth had her baby, she named him John. John grew up to be a messenger for Jesus. John told people about the Savior who was to come.

John was a little different from everybody else. He wore fuzzy clothes made out of camel's hair. He ate crunchy bugs called locusts and ate sweet, wild honey right out of the beehive.

People came from all over to hear John preach. He would stand by the Jordan River telling people that they could be forgiven for the wrong they had done. It was good news! John would baptize them right there in the Jordan River.

129

"Follow, follow me! I have good news today!
Follow, follow me! I'll show you the way!"

One day the Savior whom John had been talking about came to the Jordan River. Jesus asked John to baptize Him.

When Jesus came up out of the water, the skies opened.
They heard a voice from heaven saying, "I am so happy
to call You My Son."

After that, Jesus went into the desert to be by Himself for
forty days. But when He returned, He started preaching the
good news and looking for people to join Him in His work.

"Follow, follow Me! I have good news today!
Follow, follow Me! I'll show you the way!"

Passing a lake, Jesus walked over to some fishermen
throwing their nets into the water.

"Follow Me," Jesus told them, "and we can fish for people
instead." Right then, the brothers, Simon Peter and Andrew,
dropped their nets and followed Jesus.

Two more brothers, James and John, were on a boat getting the nets ready to fish when Jesus called, "Follow Me." They, too, left behind their work to follow Jesus.

Those four fishermen became some of Jesus' closest friends and followers. Over time, He would choose twelve men to be His closest followers, called apostles: Simon Peter, Andrew, James, John, Philip, Bartholomew, Thomas, Matthew, James (son of Alphaeus), Thaddaeus, Simon, and Judas Iscariot.

The apostles traveled everywhere with Jesus. They witnessed and wrote about many of His miracles. Jesus even gave them the power to perform miracles themselves.

During His time on earth, Jesus had many, many other followers. They spent time with Him, listening to His teachings and learning His ways. Then they would go and tell others everything that they had learned from Jesus.

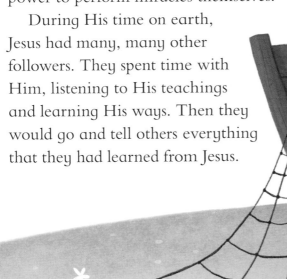

And even today, Jesus is still calling followers, to listen, to learn, and to tell others about Him.

"Follow, follow Me! Come follow Me today!
Follow, follow Me! I'll show you the Way!"

Dear Jesus, thank You for showing us the way we should go. Help us always walk in Your way. Amen.

Night night, Jesus, and Your apostles too.
May we all learn to follow, to do as You do.

Jesus Calms a Storm

Mark 4

Jesus had spent the day like any other, teaching and speaking to the crowds by the lake. Later that night, He and His followers climbed aboard a boat to cross the lake.

As the boat went farther, the skies grew darker. Thick, gray clouds covered the light of the moon. The wind began to race across the water, and the waves began to knock against the wooden boat.

Several of Jesus' friends were fishermen. They had seen sudden storms sweep across this lake before. But when the waves started coming over the sides of the boat and washing across the deck, they knew that this was no ordinary storm.

They all were thinking the same thing: *Where is Jesus?*

Whooosh goes the wind! *Craaash* go the waves!
But trust in Jesus, and you will be saved.

And that's when they found Him. He was at the back of
the boat, fast asleep.

They couldn't believe it. "Jesus!" they yelled. "Don't You
even care that we're all going to drown?"

Slowly, Jesus sat up. He looked left. He looked right. He looked up at the rain falling from the sky. Steady and sure, Jesus stood up on the rocking boat in the middle of the storm.

"Quiet!" He yelled into the wind. "Be still!" He spoke to the roaring waves.

And just like that, the wind was silent. The water was smooth as glass. The boat stood still.

The friends looked at one another. The waves and wind had stopped on command—on His command.

Again, their thoughts were the same: *Who is this Man who can even control the wind and the waves?*

Whooosh goes the wind! *Craaash* go the waves!
But trust in Jesus, and you will be saved.

Jesus looked to His friends, His followers, His disciples. "Why were you so scared?" He asked them. "Where is your faith?"

Being a follower of Jesus was really going to change the way they looked at things from now on. Yes, they would face many storms. But they would never look at the storms the same way again.

Whooosh goes the wind! *Craaash* go the waves!
But trust in Jesus, and you will be saved.

Dear Jesus, thank You for keeping me safe when life gets dark and rough. And when it does, please help me always remember to look to You. Amen.

Night night, wind, and night night, waves.
Jesus will hold me and keep me safe.

A Boy Shares His Lunch

John 6

One day Jesus and His followers had just crossed the lake, gotten off the boat, and climbed a nearby hill. Almost as soon as they had settled into the cool, green grass, Jesus looked up and saw a crowd coming. There had to be thousands of people coming to see Him.

"Those people are going to be hungry," Jesus said to Philip. "How can we feed them all?"

Philip looked out at the crowd. "Even if I worked for a whole *year*," he answered, "that money would maybe buy each person a tiny piece of bread."

But Jesus didn't need Philip's money. He already had a plan.

"Jesus!" Andrew came running over, holding a small basket. "This boy has—one, two, three, four, five—five loaves of bread and two fish!" Then Andrew looked back up at the crowd. "Oh, but that won't be enough for this many people."

So many people, so little food.
Give it to God—see what He can do!

Jesus smiled at Andrew. "Go tell everyone to find a place to sit." The other followers turned to look at Jesus, eyebrows raised. "Go on," Jesus said.

The men did what they were told. The crowd grew quieter as they found places to sit. Then everyone looked to Jesus.

But Jesus wasn't looking at the crowd. His eyes were closed as He held the bread and the fish to the heavens.

"Father, thank You for this food. And thank You for always being enough."

So many people, so little food.
Give it to God—see what He can do!

Then Jesus and His friends started passing out bread and fish to everyone who was there. No matter how many pieces of bread they tore off, no matter how many pieces of fish they handed out, there was always more to give.

And somehow those five little loaves and those two little fish lasted until the very last person was fed.

With bellies full, the people relaxed on the cool grass. Jesus and His friends looked at them all. There had to be more than five thousand people there!

"I think everyone's finished," Jesus said.

"Let's gather what's left so we don't waste anything."

Waste anything? There were only five loaves and two fish to begin with. How could there be even a tiny crumb of food left?

But again the disciples did as Jesus asked. They took baskets and gathered any food the people had left.

As the baskets came back, the disciples began to count. One, two, three, four, five . . . *twelve!* Where there had been only five loaves of bread and two little fish—after feeding more than five thousand people—there were now twelve full baskets of food.

So many people, so little food.
Give it to God—see what He can do!

Dear God, just like
the little boy with
a little lunch, I may
not have a lot
to give right now.
But please take
what I have, and
use it for Your good.
Amen.

Night night, crowd, and that little boy too.
When you give to God, He gives back to you!

Jesus Walks on Water

Matthew 14

Jesus and His followers had just fed five thousand people. But Jesus wanted to stay behind to tell the people good-bye.

"Go get in the boat," Jesus told His friends. "I'll meet you on the other side of the lake." So His friends got on a boat and pushed away from shore.

When everyone had left, Jesus walked farther into the quiet hills to pray.

Sometime later, in the middle of the night, the weather got rough on the lake. The wind was whipping, and the waves were rocking the boat. When the men looked out across the water, they couldn't believe what they saw.

"Look out there!" one of the men called.

"What is it?" another answered. They all watched the object coming across the water.

"It's—it's a ghost!" a third cried.

"Hey, it's just Me!" Jesus called to them. "Don't be scared."

"Lord, is it really You?" Peter peered out across the darkness. "If it is, call me out there to You."

A voice carried back on the wind. "Come on."

Then Peter's friends watched as he did the unthinkable. He stepped to the edge of the boat and

out into the water. But all Peter saw was Jesus. He just kept on walking until he was right there by Jesus' side.

Walk on water? In the wind and the rain?
With Jesus, we can do anything!

Peter had just done the impossible. He was standing in the middle of the lake. But with one gust of wind, Peter lost his focus.

He felt the wind on his face. He looked down at the waves lapping at his feet. He took his eyes off Jesus. And he began to sink.

Peter began flapping his arms like a helpless duck. "Help!"

Calmly, Jesus reached out a hand and lifted Peter up again. "Why would you doubt Me, Peter? Why is your faith so small?"

Then, together, Jesus and Peter walked toward the boat and climbed inside.

Their friends just shook their heads and said, "Jesus, surely You are the Son of God!"

Walk on water? In the wind and the rain?
With Jesus, we can do anything!

Dear Jesus, when
I am afraid, help
me believe in You.
And thank You for
holding me up, even
when I doubt.
Amen.

Night night, Peter, and Jesus too.
His strength is enough for me and for you!

Jesus Heals

Matthew 9; Mark 5; Luke 17

As Jesus traveled with His friends, He tried to help everyone He met. He helped minds and hearts by teaching them about God and His ways. But Jesus also helped their bodies by healing the ones who were sick.

The people had never seen someone who could heal like Jesus did. All He had to do was speak a word, and people got better. So they would come from all over to try to get Jesus to heal them.

A loving God, walking with man,
A miraculous touch, a healing hand.

One day some men picked up their friend, who was lying on a mat, and carried him all the way to Jesus. The man was paralyzed, which meant that he couldn't feel or move. And he couldn't walk to Jesus by himself.

Jesus smiled when He saw how much faith the man's friends had. He turned to the paralyzed man. "It's okay. Your sins are forgiven now."

Some of the other teachers of God's law overheard what Jesus said. *Does He think He's God?* they thought.

But Jesus even heard their thoughts and answered them. "Is it easier for Me to forgive

sins or to tell this man to walk? I will show you who I am. I have the power to forgive *and* to heal."

Then Jesus turned away from the teachers and back to the paralyzed man. "Go ahead." Jesus nodded at him. "Stand up and go home."

And the once-paralyzed man did just that.

The people watching couldn't believe it!

As Jesus continued, another man came up to Him. He bowed in front of Jesus and cried, "It's my daughter—she just died! But I know You can help me."

Jesus and His friends stopped what they were doing and went with the man toward his house. When they got there, people were outside crying.

"Why are you crying?" Jesus asked. "The girl isn't dead. She's just sleeping."

But the people laughed at Him.

Jesus and His friends got all of the people out of the house. Then Jesus went in to where the little girl lay. "Little girl," He said to her, "get up." And just like that, the little girl got up.

The girl's parents cried and held their child in their arms, forever grateful for the healing power of Jesus.

A loving God, walking with man,
A miraculous touch, a healing hand.

As Jesus was passing through a small town, ten men were there waiting for Him. They wouldn't get near Jesus because they all had a skin disease. In fact, they couldn't get near anyone until a priest said that they were cured.

"Jesus, Jesus!" they called out. "Please help us!"

Jesus turned toward them and immediately saw their illness. "Go," He replied, "and show the priest that you are healed.

The ten men turned to leave as Jesus told them to do. As they were walking, their skin became well again. They were cured!

One of the men ran all the way back to Jesus, shouting praises to God as he went. When he reached Jesus, he bowed down in front of Him. "Thank You, Jesus! Thank You!"

"Where are the rest of your friends?" Jesus asked. "There were ten of you, but only you came back to thank Me. Your belief in Me has healed you."

Not everyone was thankful for what Jesus brought to the world. But for those who accepted it—the healing, forgiving power of Jesus—their lives would never be the same.

A loving God, walking with man,
A miraculous touch, a healing hand.

Dear Jesus, thank
You for Your healing
hand. Thank You
for working miracles
for those who
believe. Amen.

Night night, Jesus, who loves us so,
Who heals us—body, heart, and soul.

Jesus Loves You

Matthew 19; Luke 18

Once a group of parents came to see Jesus with their children. They had heard about this amazing man, and they wanted Him to see their children and pray for them.

Little child, precious one,
You are loved by God's own Son.

But as the parents walked up to Jesus with their children, Jesus' disciples stopped them.

"Don't bring your children here," one disciple said to the parents, shooing them away. "Jesus is a busy man. He doesn't have time to play with a bunch of kids."

"Wait a minute," Jesus said to His disciples. And He crouched down to look the children in the eyes. "I will always, always have time for them." He ruffled a little boy's hair and smiled.

The children came toward Jesus, carefully at first. Then they began to laugh and play as Jesus talked to them and prayed with them.

"Do you see this child?" Jesus gently held the face of a young girl in His hand as He spoke to the crowd of grown-ups around Him. "This is who the kingdom of God belongs to, children like this."

Little child, precious one,
You are loved by God's own Son.

Dear Jesus, thank You for making a place for me in Your kingdom. Even when I'm a grown-up, help me always have the faith of a child. Amen.

Night night, parents, and little children too.
Jesus always has time to spend with you.

The Nice Neighbor

Luke 10

One day when Jesus was speaking, another teacher sat listening to Him. That teacher decided to test Jesus.

"So, what do I have to do to live forever?" the teacher asked.

"What does God's law say?" Jesus replied, knowing that the man already knew the answer.

"Love the Lord with all your heart, strength, and mind," the teacher answered proudly. "And love your neighbor as much as you love yourself."

"Right," Jesus said. "That's how you live forever."

Love your neighbors—it's easy to do!
Treat them the way you want them to treat you.

"But wait . . ." The teacher wasn't finished making his point. "Who exactly is my neighbor?"

Jesus took a deep breath. "Let's say a Jewish man was traveling from Jerusalem to Jericho. And while he was walking down the road, some mean guys snuck up behind him. They took all of his stuff, and they hurt him really badly.

"When a Jewish priest came down that same road, he saw the man lying there, hurt. But instead of stopping to help him, the priest walked all the way to the other side of the road and kept walking.

"Next, a Levite, another Jewish man who worked in the church, walked by. He did, at least, stop to look at the man. But then he, too, walked to the other side of the road and passed by."

Jesus continued, "Finally, another man, a Samaritan man, came by. When the Samaritan man saw the Jewish man lying on the side of the road, he went over to him and kneeled down beside him.

"'Are you okay?' the Samaritan asked. But the man could barely move. 'Don't worry. I'll take care of you.'

"The Samaritan cleaned and bandaged the man's cuts. Then he gently helped the man onto the back of his donkey and went to a nearby inn. There, he took the man inside to rest and took care of him throughout the night.

"The next morning, the Samaritan had to leave. But he told the man who owned the inn, 'Here's some money

for the room, with some extra to take care of this man. If he needs anything else, just get it for him, and I'll pay you back when I return.'"

Then Jesus looked back at the teacher. "So, which one of those men do you think acted like a neighbor?"

"The one who was nice to him," the teacher answered. "That man was his neighbor."

"Yes," Jesus agreed. "Now go and treat others the way that he did."

Love your neighbors—it's easy to do!
Treat them the way you want them to treat you.

Dear Jesus, thank You for reminding us that everyone is our neighbor. Help us always to love them the way that You do. Amen.

Night night, friends, and neighbors too.
Be nice to others; they'll be nice to you.

Jesus Washes Feet

Matthew 21; John 12–13

J esus and His friends were headed toward Jerusalem to celebrate the Passover, just like Jesus had done with His parents when He was a child.

As they got close to the city, Jesus told two of His followers to go into town and get a young donkey, called a colt, that had never been ridden before. Jesus rode that special colt.

When Jesus rode into town, the people celebrated Him like a king! They shouted praises. And they yelled, "God bless You, the One who comes in His name!"

Hosanna! Hosanna! Your praises we sing!
Save us, save us, Jesus, our King!

Although celebrating Passover was a happy time, Jesus knew that a sad time was coming. He wanted His closest followers to be ready for that sad time. So Jesus found a special place in an upstairs room to celebrate the Passover with them.

While they were having their meal, Jesus got up from the table. The followers all watched as He took off His coat and wrapped a towel around His waist. Then Jesus took a bowl of water and kneeled at Simon Peter's feet.

"Wait, Lord," Peter said, "You're not going to *wash my feet,* are You?"

Washing feet was one of the dirtiest jobs there was. Feet were *pee-eww* dirty after walking around on dusty streets in sandals all day. And washing feet was surely not a job for a leader.

Jesus looked up at Peter and said, "You will understand all of this soon."

"I don't care!" Peter said, pulling his feet back away from Jesus. "You will *never* wash my feet."

"Well, then," Jesus said simply, "you are not My follower."

Peter looked at Jesus, wide-eyed. Then he lowered his feet into Jesus' hands. "In that case, please, wash my hands and head too!"

Then one by one, foot by foot, toe by little toe, Jesus washed His apostles' feet. Jesus had entered Jerusalem like a king. Now He was doing the job of the lowliest servant for His followers.

After He finished, He asked, "Do you know why I washed your feet?"

The disciples just listened in silence. They still didn't know what to say. No teacher, much less a *king,* had ever done what Jesus had just done."Yes, I am your Teacher. Yes, I am your Lord. And, yes, I have also washed your feet. This is exactly what you should do. Serve each other the way I have served you."

Hosanna! Hosanna! Your praises we sing!
You are like no other, Jesus, our King!

Dear Jesus, thank You for showing us how to lead and love others. Help us always serve like You. Amen.

Night night, disciples, and Jesus too.
May we all learn to serve like You.

Jesus Lives

Matthew 26–28; Mark 16; Luke 24

After Jesus' dinner with His followers, He went to the garden to pray. He knew that it was almost time for trouble to start. While He was praying, men came with swords and clubs to arrest Him.

One of Jesus' followers pulled out a sword to try to defend Him. But Jesus said, "Put your sword away. I could ask My Father to help Me if I wanted. But this must happen as God's Word says."

Then Jesus was taken to the leaders. They asked for people to come up and tell them what Jesus had done wrong. Then they asked Jesus Himself.

"Tell us, are You really the Son of God?"

177

"Yes," Jesus answered, "I am."

That was all they needed. That was enough to punish Jesus. Then the leaders stirred up the people against Jesus. And the people started yelling, "Crucify Him, crucify Him!"

And with that, they killed Jesus. The miraculous Healer, amazing Teacher, Servant to all, and Son of God was sent to die on a big, wooden cross.

When Jesus took His last breath, the earth rumbled. The sky grew dark. And the soldiers whispered, "He really *was* the Son of God."

Jesus' followers took His body, wrapped it in cloths, and laid it in a tomb. Then they rolled a huge stone over the opening. And the followers walked away, trying to figure out how they had lost the best Teacher, the best Friend, and the only Savior they had ever known. But the good news—the best news, for you and me, and for us all—is that wasn't the end of the story.

On the third day after Jesus died on that cross, His mother, Mary, and another follower named Mary Magdalene went back to Jesus' tomb. But they didn't see Jesus. They saw an angel. And the great big stone that covered the tomb had been rolled away.

"I know who you're looking for," the angel said with a smile. "But He isn't here. He is *alive!*"

Jesus is alive! He lives again!
He was God's plan—to save us from sin.

The women ran back to tell the other followers. And soon, they all saw it for themselves. It was true.

Jesus was alive.

It had been God's plan all along. When Jesus suffered on that big wooden cross and shook the world with His death, He paid the price for our sins. And all of our sins died on the cross with Him that day.

Jesus beat sin. He beat death. And He came back again to show His followers the truth: He is alive. And He offers that same precious life to us all if we choose to accept Him.

Jesus is alive! He lives again!
He was God's plan—to save us from sin.

Dear Jesus, thank
You for giving Your
life to save mine.
Thank You for
forgiving all my
sins. Amen.

Night night, Jesus, sent from God above.
You saved us with Your life and Your love.

Go Tell the World!

Matthew 28; Luke 24; Acts 1

After Jesus rose back to life, His *resurrection,* He spent some time with His disciples. He ate with them and talked with them and explained to them what had happened. He told them why He had to be hurt and killed. "God's Word says that the Savior must die," Jesus told them. "It also says that He would rise again three days later. And you all saw that happen."

The disciples nodded with a smile, still amazed at all that they had seen and heard.

"Now you must go tell other people about it," Jesus told them. "If people will listen and change their lives and follow Me, their sins will be forgiven. They will be saved."

Go, go, tell the good news!
Jesus Christ died to save me and you!

Jesus spent forty days with His disciples. But then it was time for Jesus to go back to His home in heaven. Together, He and His disciples went to a mountain to say good-bye.

Jesus knew this was the last time He would be face to face with His disciples on earth for a while. And Jesus had some very important words to tell them before He left.

He said...

"Go, tell everyone this good news you've seen and heard.

"Go, teach them and help them follow Me.

"Go, baptize them in the name of the Father, the Son, and the Holy Spirit.

"Go, into all the world.

"And I will be with you wherever you go."

With those words, Jesus began to lift off the ground. He rose and rose and rose into the sky, into the clouds, until His disciples, His followers, His friends from this earth could see Him no more.

But they knew that He was still there, still in their hearts, still Immanuel, still "God with us." And they knew that He would always be there—*always*—wherever they may go.

Go, go, tell the good news!
Jesus Christ lives to save me and you!

Dear Jesus, thank
You for bringing
good news for us all.
Help me as I go into
the world and share
with others the
good news of You.
Amen.

Night night, Jesus, who loves me so,
Who will be with me wherever I go.

Pictures of Heaven

Revelation 1; 21

Many years after Jesus had gone back to heaven, the apostle John had grown old and gray. John had been one of Jesus' first followers, one of the brothers whom Jesus had called from their fishing boat.

Even now, John was still being a fisher of men. He was still telling others about Jesus, as Jesus had asked His followers to do. But that had gotten John punished. He had been sent away to live on an island all by himself.

While John was there, on the island of Patmos, a very special visitor took him to a very special place.

A new heaven and earth,
treasures untold,
Walking with God
down streets made of gold.

One day John heard a voice like a trumpet. The voice told John to write down what he saw and give what he had written to the churches. Then John turned around and saw Jesus standing there. But this time, Jesus wasn't like any man John had ever seen. His hair was as white as snow. There were flames in His eyes. And His feet were like hot, glowing metal.

"Don't be afraid," Jesus said to His old friend John. "I am the First, the Last, and the One who lives forever."

Then Jesus took John to show him many things that were to come.

John saw a whole new heaven and a whole new earth. God will live there with His people. All the bad things of this world—death, sadness, crying, pain—they will all be gone. God will wipe them all away.

Then John saw Jesus sitting on a throne. Jesus said, "Write this down. Tell everyone. I am making everything brand-new!"

After that, John was taken to a beautiful, shining city. The whole city was made of gold and sparkling jewels. There were huge gates, and each gate was made from one white, shimmery pearl. Even the streets were made of pure gold.

There was no sun and no moon in this place. God's holy light shined throughout the city, lighting it just as if it were daytime. And it was all the light that the city would ever need.

This city of gold was a place made for God's people, those who believed in Jesus.

As John's tour of the city ended, Jesus said to John, "I will come back soon for everyone! Watch for Me. And to anyone who is thirsty, come to Me. I will give you the water of life."

A new heaven and earth, treasures untold,
Walking with God down streets made of gold.

Dear heavenly Father, thank You for all Your promises. Thank You for making me a beautiful home where I can live with You forever. Amen.

Night night, Jesus, making all things new,
With a heavenly home for me and for you.

About the Author

Amy Parker's children's books have sold more than a million copies, including two Christian Retailing's Best award-winning books and the bestselling *A Night Night Prayer*; *Night Night, Farm*; and *Night Night, Train*. She lives outside Nashville with her husband and two children.

About the Illustrator

Virginia Allyn has illustrated more than a dozen children's books. She lives above a chocolate shop in a beautiful New Hampshire village. She enjoys collecting children's books, hiking, and eating all her vegetables (except peas).

Other Night Night books by
Amy Parker

9780718088316

9780718089320

9781400310036

9780718090869

9780718042462

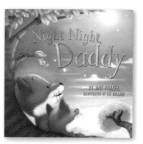

9780718042301

9781400318254

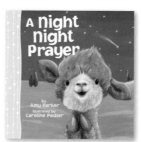

9781400324316